DoD 1000.21-R

Department of Defense

I0426064

# Passport
# and
# Passport Agent Services
# Regulation

## April 1997

Director of Administration and Management,
Office of the Secretary of Defense

**OFFICE OF THE SECRETARY OF DEFENSE**
1950 DEFENSE PENTAGON
WASHINGTON, DC 20301-1950

ADMINISTRATION &/
MANAGEMENT

# FOREWORD

This Regulation is reissued under the authority of DoD Directive 1000.21, "DoD Passport and Passport Agent Services," July 9, 1992. It provides guidance for administration of Passport and Passport Agent Services. It also provides guidance on the preparation of required documents for the acquisition and control of no-fee passport and/or visas necessary for official travel. Finally, it prescribes the use of DD Form 1056, "Authorization to Apply for a No-Fee Passport and/or Request for Visa," by all the DoD Components. The Department of State (DoS) forms authorized for use by the DoS Passport Agent's Manual are prescribed by this Regulation for use by all the DoD Components. Military passport agents will utilize these forms to fulfill DoS requirements for information needed for processing passports and passport applications. DoD 1000.21-R, "Passport and Passport Agent Services Regulation," August 1992, is hereby canceled.

This Regulation applies to the Office of the Secretary of Defense (OSD), the Military Departments, the Chairman of the Joint Chiefs of Staff, the Combatant Commands, and the Defense Agencies (hereafter referred to collectively as "the DoD Components". The term "Military Services," as used herein, refers to the Army, the Navy, the Air Force, and the Marine Corps.

This Regulation is effective immediately and is mandatory for use by all the DoD Components. The Heads of the DoD Components may issue supplementary instructions only when necessary to provide for unique requirements within their DoD Component. All implementation documents and supplementary instructions must be approved by the Executive Agent before publication.

Send recommended changes to the Regulation to:

Administrative Assistant to the Secretary of the Army
105 Army Pentagon
Washington, DC 20310-0105

The DoD Components may obtain copies of this Regulation through their own publications channels. Approved for public release; distribution unlimited. Authorized registered users may obtain copies of this Regulation from Defense Technical Information Center, 8725 John J. Kingman Rd., STE 0944, Ft. Belvoir, VA 22060-6218. Other Federal Agencies and the public may obtain copies from the U.S. Department of Commerce, National Technical Information Service, 5285 Port Royal Road, Springfield, VA 22161.

D. O. COOKE
Director

# TABLE OF CONTENTS

Page

FOREWORD                                                                                    2

TABLE OF CONTENTS                                                                           3

FIGURES                                                                                     4

REFERENCES                                                                                  5

CHAPTER 1.  -  GENERAL INFORMATION                                                          6

    C1.1.  Purpose                                                      6
    C1.2.  Definitions                                                  6
    C1.3.  Policy                                                       8
    C1.4.  Responsibilities                                             9
    C1.5.  Use of Passports                                             15
    C1.6.  Validity of Passports                                        17
    C1.7.  Determination of Passport and Visa Requirements              17
    C1.8.  Alien DoD Personnel and Alien Family Members                 17
    C1.9.  Stateless Aliens                                             18

CHAPTER 2.  -  PASSPORT AND VISA APPLICATION PROCEDURES                                     19

    C2.1.  Applying for a Passport (with or without visa(s))             19
    C2.2.  Applying for a Visa                                          25
    C2.3.  Completion of DD Form 1056, "Authorization to Apply for a No-Fee Passport and/or      28
Request for Visa"
    C2.4.  Processing Passport and/or Visa Applications                 31

CHAPTER 3.  -  PASSPORT AGENT NOMINATION AND DESIGNATION PROCEDURES                         36

    C3.1.  Passport Agent Nominations                                   36
    C3.2.  Passport Agent Designation Procedures                        36
    C3.3.  Reglar Fee Passport Applications                             38

CHAPTER 4.  -  QUALITY CONTROL, DISTRIBUTION, AND DISPOSITION                               39

    C4.1.  Quality Checks                                               39
    C4.2.  Control                                                      39
    C4.3.  Distribution                                                 41
    C4.4.  Disposition                                                  42

CHAPTER 5.  -  REQUIRED FORMS AND PUBLICATIONS                                              46

    C5.1.  Required DoD Form                                            46
    C5.2.  Required DoS Forms (DPS Forms)                               46
    C5.3.  Required DoD and DoS Publications                            47

# FIGURES

| Figure | Title | Page |
|--------|-------|------|
| C2.F1. | Passport and/or Visa Appication Assembly | 20 |
| C2.F2. | Incoming Distribution (Passport and/or Visa Applications) | 21 |
| C2.F3. | DD Form 1056, "Authorization to Apply for a "No-Fee" Passport and/or Request for Visa," for Service Member | 34 |
| C2.F4. | DD Form 1056, "Authorization to Apply for a "No-Fee" Passport and/or Request for Visa," for Family Member | 35 |
| C3.F1. | Sample Agent Appointment and/or Cancellation Request | 37 |
| C3.F2. | Military Office of Responsibility (OPR) | 38 |

TABLE OF CONTENTS/FIGURES

# REFERENCES

(a) DoD Directive 1000.21, "DoD Passport and Passport Agent Services," July 9, 1992

(b) United States Department of State Passport Agent's Manual

(c) DoD 4500.54-G, "Foreign Clearance Guide (FCG)," January 1992, authorized by DoD Directive 4500.54, May 1, 1991

(d) Title 22, Code of Federal Regulations, Part 51, "Passports," current edition

(e) Section 1543 of title 18, United States Code

(f) Modification of the March 25, 1991 Memorandum of Agreement (MOA) between the Department of Defense and Department of State, October 15, 1996

(g) Joint Federal Travel Regulations (JFTR), Volume 1, "Uniformed Service Members," current edition

(h) Article 136, Uniform Code of Mlitary Justice

(i) Section 936 of title 10, United States Code

(j) Section 2903 of title 5, United States Code

(k) Memorandum of Agreement (MOA) between the Department of Defense and Department of State, August 13, 1993

## C1. CHAPTER 1

## GENERAL INFORMATION

### C1.1. PURPOSE

This Regulation implements DoD Directive 1000.21 (reference (a)) and establishes DoD and Department of State (DoS) policies and procedures for obtaining no-fee passports and/or visas and administration of Passport and Passport Agent Services. This Regulation is used in conjunction with the DoS Passport Agent's Manual (reference (b)) and the Department of Defense Foreign Clearance Guide (FCG) (reference (c)). It provides instructions and control of forms required for passports and/or visa applications and prescribes the use for DD Form 1056, "Authorization to Apply for a No-Fee Passport and/or Visa." It specifies DoS and DoD policy and procedural guidance on the acquisition, issuance, and use of passports and/or visas for official travel.

### C1.2. DEFINTIONS

C1.2.1. Passport Agent. A person authorized and empowered by the Secretary of State, the DoD Executive Agent (for DoD Passport and Passport Agent Services), or the Secretaries of the Military Departments to accept passport applications and perform passport services to include administering oaths for passport purposes (22 CFR 51.21(c), reference (d)).

C1.2.2. DoD Executive Agent. The Head of a DoD Component delegated to administer a function or service for others in the Department of Defense on behalf of the Secretary of Defense. Reference (a) designates the Secretary of the Army as Executive Agent for Passport and Passport Agent Services. The Administrative Assistant to the Secretary of the Army acts for the Secretary of the Army in executing the Secretary of the Army's responsibilities as the Executive Agent.

C1.2.3. DoD Foreign Clearance Guide (FCG) (Reference (c)). A reference document containing detailed information on special travel areas, foreign country entrance requirements, and overseas commanders' requirements on visits within their area of command.

C1.2.4. DoD Passport Agent Services. Includes, but is not limited to, processing passport agent designations, duties, training, and responsibilities.

C1.2.5. <u>DoD Passport Services</u>.   Includes, but is not limited to processing applications for no-fee passports and visas and distribution and control of no-fee passports and visas.

C1.2.6. <u>Installation</u>.   A grouping of facilities, located in the same vicinity, which support particular functions where passport agents operate and provide passport services to DoD personnel and family members.   For purposes of this regulation, the term installation is used as a generic term used to identify a military base, post, camp, depot, etc.

C1.2.7. <u>Minor Child</u>.   For passport purposes, a minor is an unmarried person under the age of 18.

C1.2.8. <u>Office of Primary Responsibility (OPR)</u>.   The designated office responsible for compliance with governing passport and visa regulations and directives, issuance of implementing instructions, and management of passport services within each of the Military Departments.

C1.2.9. <u>Official Travel</u>.   Authorized travel and assignment solely in connection with official business of the Department of Defense and the U.S. Government at Government expense.

C1.2.10. <u>Passport</u>.   An internationally recognized travel document attesting to the identity and nationality of the bearer.   A passport indicates that its bearer is entitled to receive the protection and assistance of the diplomatic and consular offices of their country while abroad.   In essence, it is a request on the part of the issuing government that officials of foreign governments permit the bearer to travel or sojourn in their territories and afford them lawful aid and protection.

C1.2.10.1. <u>U.S. Passports as Government Property</u>.   The U.S. passport is an official document of the U.S. Government.   It remains at all times the property of the United States and must be returned to the Government upon demand.   It may not be altered, mutilated, or changed in any manner, except as authorized and changed by DoS Passport Services or its agencies, or by a consular post abroad upon proper authorization from DoS Passport Services.   Anyone who mutilates or makes an unauthorized change of a passport is subject to criminal penalties (18 U.S.C. 1543, reference (e)).

C1.2.10.2. <u>No-Fee Passports</u>.   Passports issued to DoD personnel and their family members carrying out official duties.   The no-fee passport carries an endorsement that identifies the bearer is an agent of the U.S. Government proceeding abroad on official travel. This endorsement is unique to no-fee passports. Passports are provided by the Government at Government expense; hence, no-fee to the passport applicant. The types of no-fee passports provided for official travel are: diplomatic (black), official (maroon), and no-fee regular (blue and/or green). No-fee passports are normally valid for 5 years.

C1.2.11. <u>Regional Passport Agencies</u>. A network of the DoS agencies established within 14 geographical areas that issues fee passports to the general public. All no-fee (blue and/or green) passport applications must be processed at the Washington Regional Passport Agency. The only exception is the DoS agency in Honolulu. The Honolulu Region consists of American Samoa, the Federated States of Micronesia, Guam, Hawaii, and the Northern Mariana Islands (Saipan, Rota, and Tinian). Passport agents must verify with the DoS Regional Agency in their area whether dependent passports can be processed on a case by case situation based on an emergency. A complete listing of regional territories and agency addresses can be found in the DoS Passport Agent's Manual. The Washington Regional Passport Agency is the only agency authorized to issue official and diplomatic passports.

C1.2.12. <u>Visa</u>. A stamp or impression placed on a page of a valid passport by a foreign embassy or consulate empowered to grant permission, as of the date issued, for the applicant to enter and remain in that country for a specific period of time. (Period of validity varies by country.)

C1.3. <u>POLICY</u>

It is DoD policy under the MOA (reference (f)) to:

C1.3.1. Designate only U.S. citizens as passport agents.

C1.3.2. Designate, in writing, DoD employees to serve as DoD passport agents.

C1.3.3. Specify, in writing, the functions and responsibilities of civilian and/or Military personnel serving as DoD passport agents, consistent with reference (f).

C1.3.4. Ensure that designated passport agents:

C1.3.4.1. Perform all services required by the DoS for the acceptance of passport applications in accordance with the DoS Passport Agent's Manual, the FCG (reference (c)), periodic supplemental instructions issued by the DoS Passport

Services, and other DoD Component supplemental instructions as approved by the DoD Executive Agent.

C1.3.4.2.  Comply with and maintain this regulation, the DoS Passport Agent's Manual (reference (b)) and reference (c).

C1.3.4.3.  Decline the processing of regular fee passport applications, unless specifically approved by the Department of Defense and the DoS in writing. (See Chapter 3., section C3.3.)

C1.3.5.  Distribute, upon request, DoS-supplied passport information, materials, and forms, as may be required.

C1.3.6.  Ensure that DoD personnel:

C1.3.6.1.  Traveling abroad, on official business, are in possession of the proper no-fee passport (either diplomatic, official or no-fee regular) and appropriate visa(s); are briefed that passports are the property of the U.S. Government, not to be used for personal travel; and are briefed that passports shall be surrendered to the Government on demand by an authorized representative of the U.S. Government.

C1.3.6.2.  Safeguard passports as sensitive items.


## C1.4.  RESPONSIBILITIES

C1.4.1.  As delegated by the DoD Executive Agent for Passport and Passport Agent Services, the Administrative Assistant to the Secretary if the Army, shall:

C1.4.1.1.  Administer DoD Passport and Passport Agent Services.

C1.4.1.2.  Designate, in writing, individual DoD passport agents.

C1.4.1.3.  Obtain names of individuals from all DoD Components who will serve as points of contact to disseminate information on Passports and Passport Agent Services.

C1.4.1.4.  Provide passport agent training programs consistent with DoD and DoS guidelines, and the DoS Passport Agent's Manual.   (See Chapter 3., section C3.3.)

C1.4.1.5.  Annually, review DoD Passport and Passport Agent Services with the DoS Components' points of contact (POCS) and the Military Departments' OPR representatives.

C1.4.1.6.  Annually, review DoD Passport and Passport Agent Services with the DoS; and maintain liaison with DoS on policies about Passports and Passport Agent Services.

C1.4.2.  For the DoD Components requiring passport agents, the Heads of the DoD Components (less the Military Departments), shall:

C1.4.2.1.  Establish Passport and Passport Agent Services that conform to the requirements contained in the DoS Passport Agent's Manual, DoD guidelines, and the DoD FCG.

C1.4.2.2.  Inform travelers en route to, or traveling through, DoD-designated high or potential security threat countries of the DoD travel security policy, specifically as it relates to the use of and requirements for passports.

C1.4.2.3.  Designate, in writing, passport agents in accordance with the guidelines in this Regulation.

C1.4.2.4.  Ensure passport agents are fully trained before assumption of duties and, upon designation, are available to serve a minimum of 1 year.

C1.4.2.5.  Maintain an adequate supply of DoS and DoD publications and forms.

C1.4.2.6.  Designate, in writing, a POC to issue policy and guidance for that Component's role in the DoD Passport and Passport Agent Services program.  The POC serves as that DoD Component's focal point for obtaining, reviewing, and providing information to the DoD Executive Agent.

C1.4.2.7.  Nominate only permanently assigned DoD civilian employees and/or Military personnel to become passport agents.

C1.4.2.8.  Request authorization to accept fee passport applications, only in very unusual circumstances.  Requests for exception to DoS policy must be forwarded through the Service OPR to the DoD Executive Agent.  The DoD Executive Agent will coordinate the request with DoS.  See Chapter 3., section 3.3., for submission.

C1.4.3. The <u>Secretaries of the Military Departments</u> shall:

C1.4.3.1. Designate an OPR to serve as that Military Service's focal point for obtaining, reviewing, and providing information to the DoD Executive Agent.

C1.4.3.2. Provide a representative from their respective OPR to annually review their Passport and Passport Agent Services at a place specified by the DoD Executive Agent.

C1.4.3.3. Designate passport agents in writing. (See Chapter 3.)

C1.4.4. The <u>U.S. Army Service Center for the Armed Forces</u> shall:

C1.4.4.1. Receive and execute DoD passport applications.

C1.4.4.2. Receive passports from the DoS for the DoD Components.

C1.4.4.3. Process visa requests for the DoD Components.

C1.4.4.4. Return passports to the DoD Components' passport agents.

C1.4.4.5. Assist DoD alien family members in obtaining visas for official travel.

C1.4.4.6. Respond to passport agents inquiries on passport or visa processing.

C1.4.4.7. Serve as liaison with the DoS on procedural and/or policy matters relating to passport services.

C1.4.5. The <u>Major Military Commands Outside the U.S.</u> shall:

C1.4.5.1. Coordinate directly with U.S. Embassies and Consulates to establish procedures for obtaining passports and visas for official travel of DoD personnel and their family members.

C1.4.5.2. Designate, in writing, passport agents and/or military couriers. Agents and/or couriers may accept and process passport and visa applications in accordance with instructions issued by their servicing U.S. Embassy and/or Consulate, the overseas command and this Regulation.

C1.4.6. The <u>Installation and/or Activity Commanders</u> shall:

C1.4.6.1.  Ensure personnel on official travel are informed of passport and visa requirements, as specified by the FCG.

C1.4.6.2.  Provide command emphasis on efficient passport and visa application processing to avert port call delays and adverse effects on mission accomplishments.

C1.4.6.3.  Ensure subordinate commands and activities designate in writing authorizing officials to sign DD Form 1056, "Authorization to Apply for a No-Fee Passport and/or Request for Visa."  A copy of the designation shall be kept on file by installation passport agents.

C1.4.6.4.  Ensure all passport agents are trained in their duties and responsibilities as prescribed in the DoS Passport Agent's Manual and governing regulations.

C1.4.7.  The <u>DD Form 1056 Authorizing Official</u> shall:

C1.4.7.1.  Verify applicants listed on the DD Form 1056 are authorized official travel status (awaiting orders) and therefore are authorized to apply for and use a no-fee passport and visa for official travel.

C1.4.7.2.  Advise applicants that regular-fee passports cannot be used in place of no-fee passports, nor can no-fee passports be used in place of regular-fee passports.  Countries can deny entry or detain travelers if their passport does not indicate their actual travel status.

C1.4.7.3.  Prepare or oversee the preparation of DD Form 1056.

C1.4.7.4.  Authenticate DD Form 1056 with their signature in Item 16.

C1.4.7.5.  Direct applicants to the proper passport agent for completing and processing passport applications.

C1.4.8.  The <u>Passport Agent</u> shall:

C1.4.8.1.  Comply with this Regulation, appropriate Military Service guidance, and the DoS Passport Agent's Manual (reference (b)).  Maintain the current edition of the FCG and be on the mailing list for changes and/or updates.

C1.4.8.2.  Maintain a file copy of agent approval issued by the Military Service OPR.

C1.4.8.3.  Prepare DD Form 1056 when a no-fee passport and/or visa is required.  See Chapter 2., section C2.3., for information on the use and processing of DD Form 1056.

C1.4.8.4.  Ensure DD Form 1056 is accurately completed and properly authenticated.  If serving as the DD Form 1056 Authorizing Official, verify applicant's official travel status.

C1.4.8.5.  Require each passport applicant to complete a DoS passport application.

C1.4.8.6.  Establish the identity of the passport applicant and record identification in accordance with Chapter 7 of the DoS Passport Agent's Manual (reference (b)).  Establishing identity and recording this information is the most important function of the passport agent.

C1.4.8.7.  Review citizenship evidence, Chapter 5 of reference (b).

C1.4.8.8.  For personal security reasons, do not process passport photographs in which Military, or Military-like, uniforms or clothing are being worn by the applicant.

C1.4.8.9.  Execute passport applications in accordance with Chapter 9 of reference (b).

C1.4.8.10.  Assemble and post passport and/or visa application packets for mailing to the designated processing office each duty day.  (See Chapter 2., Figure C2.F1.)

C1.4.8.11.  Assist applicants in preparing visa applications when the forms must be completed personally by the applicant.

C1.4.8.12.  Coordinate short notice requests for passports with United States Army Service Center for the Armed Forces (USASCAF).

C1.4.8.13.  Maintain a suspense control system for passport and visa applications.

C1.4.8.14. Trace applications status as required, via message, telefax or phone call.

C1.4.8.15. Take corrective action, within 48 hours, on application discrepancy letters received from an OPR or the DoS.

C1.4.8.16. Maintain accountability of passports when not currently issued to individual applicants for official travel.

C1.4.8.17. Cancel and or destroy no-fee passports when they are no longer needed. (See Chapter 4., subsection C4.4.5.and subsection C4.4.6.)

C1.4.8.18. Advise applicants:

C1.4.8.18.1. How and where to obtain birth certificates. A DoS Information Sheet M-343, "Notice to Applicant Concerning Birth Records," shall be provided to each applicant that contains a form for their use in obtaining birth records. Normally, applicants receive better service from vital statistics offices when Information Sheet M-343 is used.

C1.4.8.18.2. When and where to apply for passports.

C1.4.8.18.3. That DoD personnel and their family members should complete passport applications and receive necessary passport and/or visa(s) before departing their installation.

C1.4.8.18.4. That it takes 45 to 60 days for passport and/or visa processing.

C1.4.8.18.5. That the passport agent shall receive the passport and is responsible for passport delivery to each applicant. Normally, passports will not be sent directly to a leave address or ports of embarkation. However, on short notice movements an exception to policy may be granted by the OPR. Applicants must be in possession of both passport and visa(s) before travel arrangements may be processed.

C1.4.8.18.6. Of the responsibilities in subsection C1.4.10., below.

C1.4.8.18.7. That the passport must be signed in black ink, immediately upon receipt.

C1.4.8.18.8. That the passport is for official travel purposes only.

C1.4.8.18.9. That the passport is the property of the U.S. Government and may be recalled at any time by proper authority.

C1.4.9. <u>The Installation, Activity, and/or Unit Commander</u> shall: Maintain control and/or accountability of no-fee passports issued to assigned personnel. No-fee passports must be maintained in a secure manner and issued to individuals as needed for official travel only. Upon completion of travel, no-fee passports shall be maintained in the unit for safe-keeping. Units must return passports to the passport agent for cancellation and/or destruction once they are no longer required or expire.

C1.4.10. <u>Applicant must</u>:

C1.4.10.1. Establish his and/or her identity to the passport agent's satisfaction.

C1.4.10.1.1. Military personnel and their family members authorized a military identification card must present their identification cards.

C1.4.10.1.2. DoD civilian personnel, and their family members, must present DoD civilian identification cards, if available, or other acceptable documents in accordance with Chapter 7, DoS Passport Agent's Manual (reference (b)).

C1.4.10.1.3. A parent's identification card must be shown whenever a parent signs and/or executes an application for a minor child under age 13. A parent, legal guardian, or person in loco parentis, whether a U.S. citizen or not, must personally appear and execute an application for a child less than 13 years of age. If a legal guardian or person in loco parentis executes an application on behalf of a child, under age 13, documentation of guardianship or a notarized statement from the parent or legal authority giving them permission to execute the application on behalf of the child must be shown to the passport agent.

C1.4.10.2. Applicants must submit proper evidence of U.S. citizenship with each passport application in accordance with Chapter 3, of reference (b).

## C1.5. USE OF PASSPORTS

C1.5.1. No-fee passports are used by eligible DoD personnel and their family members while on official travel to countries requiring passports. Each family member must obtain a separate no-fee passport regardless of his or her age. Family

CHAPTER 1

members must have no-fee passports in their possession before port call. No-fee passports are issued for a specific purpose and may be used only under the conditions or restrictions specified. To expedite passport processing, all members of the Armed Forces and family members should have a certified copy of their birth certificate with a raised seal or a previously issued passport.

C1.5.1.1. DoD personnel and family members assigned within the United States, each must obtain a regular-fee passport for personal travel abroad. Visas required for personal travel are the responsibility of the traveler.

C1.5.1.2. While outside the United States, no-fee passports may be used for incidental personal travel between foreign destinations providing the foreign government concerned accepts no-fee passports for personal travel. If the foreign government does not accept no-fee passports for personal travel, travelers must obtain regular-fee passports at their own expense.

C1.5.2. To enhance the travel security of DoD personnel and family members on official orders to and/or from high or potential physical threat countries by commercial conveyance (bus, train, plane) or private auto, the Department of Defense has authorized the option of allowing these travelers to obtain and use (in addition to their official or diplomatic passport) the regular-fee (tourist (blue and/or green)) passport. This option is exercised for security reasons only, and is not to be considered a requirement. Travelers wishing to obtain regular-fee passports in addition to their official, diplomatic, or no-fee regular passport are responsible for obtaining their own regular-fee passports and required visas.

C1.5.2.1. Reimbursement for passports and visas obtained under these conditions is authorized by the Joint Federal Travel Regulations (JFTR U4525 and JFTR U5212) (reference (g)). Payment is made upon submission of paid receipts and/or canceled checks submitted with the travel voucher.

C1.5.2.2. Individuals traveling solely by the Air Mobility Command or charter are not reimbursed for regular-fee passports, unless U.S. Government transportation became available on short notice (i.e., after commercial travel arrangements had been made and passport purchased), or priority of travel is sufficiently high to require backup travel arrangements.

C1.5.2.3. Reimbursement for regular-fee passports for personal travel is not authorized.

C1.5.3. Military officers in grade O-7 and above are authorized to apply for and use no-fee passports when on official travel outside the continental United States regardless of the requirements outlined in the FCG.

## C1.6. VALIDITY OF PASSPORTS

C1.6.1. A passport is valid only when signed by or for the bearer in the proper space.

C1.6.2. Unless specifically limited to a shorter validity period, no-fee passports are valid for 5 years from date of issue.

## C1.7. DETERMINATION OF PASSPORT AND VISA REQUIREMENTS

C1.7.1. The FCG is the authority for travel clearance, passport, and visas requirements for DoD personnel and their family members to enter foreign countries on official business. DoS uses the FCG in approving the issuance of no-fee passports.

C1.7.2. Reassignment orders will include passport and visa requirements in the special assignment instructions. DoS makes final determination on the type of no-fee passport to be issued for overseas assignments based on the FCG, traveler's duty assignment, and destination shown on DD Form 1056 and official orders.

## C1.8. ALIEN DoD PERSONNEL AND ALIEN FAMILY MEMBERS

C1.8.1. Alien family members are not eligible to obtain and use U.S. passports. These individuals must apply for and obtain passports from the countries in which they claim citizenship.

C1.8.2. DoD personnel and family members who are not U.S. citizens must maintain a current passport from the country in which they claim citizenship.

C1.8.3. Individuals are responsible for documentation required for departing or entering the United States on official travel. Entry to and exit from the United States of alien family members is strictly a matter between the individual, the U.S. Immigration and Naturalization Service (INS), and the DoS. Individuals must work with the INS to ensure proper documentation for departure from and return to the United States.

C1.8.4. Alien DoD personnel and family members should contact their local passport agents, who will contact USASCAF or OPR to obtain information on the current visa requirements.

C1.8.5. For official travel only, USASCAF or appropriate OPR shall obtain required visas for valid alien passport, provided the alien is within the United States. Passports must be current and must be valid for at least 1 year. For further information on passport validity, the individual should contact a Consulate or the Embassy of the nation concerned.

C1.8.6. Alien personnel outside the United States should contact the U.S. Embassy or Consulate to obtain visa requirements.

C1.8.7. Application processing time for alien visas varies by country. Initiate applications immediately after assignment confirmation. Passport agents must follow procedures in Chapter 2. when assembling alien visa applications. Only use accountable mail when forwarding alien passports for visa processing. Forward a applications in accordance with Figure C2.F2.

## C1.9. STATELESS ALIENS

C1.9.1. Stateless aliens and aliens whose countries are without Consular or Diplomatic representation in the U.S. must contact the INS office to obtain proper travel documents.

C1.9.2. Valid reentry permits or other alien travel documents used instead of a foreign passport must be sent to USASCAF or appropriate OPR with a completed DD Form 1056. The USASCAF or appropriate OPR obtains visas from the embassies.

## C2. CHAPTER 2

## PASSPORT AND VISA APPLICATION PROCEDURES

### C2.1. APPLYING FOR A PASSPORT (WITH OR WITHOUT VISA(S))

#### C2.1.1. When to Apply for a Passport

##### C2.1.1.1. Permanent Change of Station (PCS)

C2.1.1.1.1. DoD personnel requiring no-fee passports should apply immediately, but not later than 14 days after reassignment notification. Personnel should not wait for orders to be published before submitting passport applications. A memorandum of intent, instruction, or message may be submitted to avoid delays. Applications for diplomatic passports, however, may not be issued until orders or written assignment instructions are submitted.

C2.1.1.1.2. Family members of military personnel should apply within 14 days of the Service member electing to serve a "with dependents" tour. Applications should not be delayed because they are waiting for orders to be published or for approval of family travel.

C2.1.1.1.3. Family members of DoD civilians should apply with their sponsor.

C2.1.1.2. Temporary Duty (TDY and/or TAD). DoD personnel should apply as soon as travel requirements are identified.

C2.1.1.3. Overseas. DoD personnel who acquire new family members while abroad or have passports that will expire before their scheduled return to the United States must apply for new passports through their installation and/or activity to the servicing Embassy or Consulate.

#### C2.1.2. How to Obtain a No-Fee Passport

C2.1.2.1. Each DoD personnel and family member must submit a DD Form 1056 and supporting documents as part of their passport applications for official travel. DD Form 1056 should be completed by the appropriate office handling travel arrangements. In addition to the DD Form 1056, the "DoS Application for Passport,"

(DSP Form 11) or "Application for Passport by Mail," (DSP Form 82) must be completed by the applicant.

    C2.1.2.2.  Passport agent must properly assemble applications and mail. (See Figures C2.F1. and C2.F2.).

Figure C2.F1.  <u>PASSPORT AND/OR VISA APPLICATION ASSEMBLY</u>

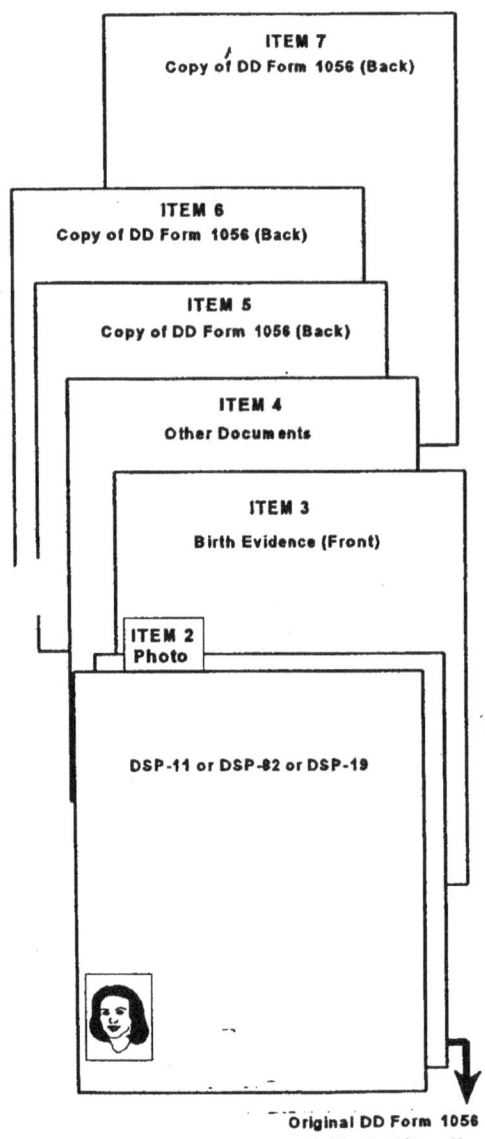

*Staple photo to application with four staples (one in each corner, do not damage facial features).*

Item 1 - Attach the following documents behind the application, in the order listed:  Original DD Form 1056 stapled to item 1.  Should be head to head, facing forward on the back of DSP - 11/82.  Place a stapled in the left and right margins, three inches down from the top and one-quarter inch in from the sides.

Item 2 - Affix a second photo to the passport: *Place upside down, facing forward, between the application and the DD Form 1056, so facial features are not damaged (staple added after all documents are placed).*

Item 3 - Place birth/citizenship evidence, opened and facing forward for easy reading. *When using a passport, open to the data page and staple the thinnest edge of the book to the application.*

Item 4 - Attach other documents and/or statements from the applicant or agent; DSP 64, orders, visas forms, and affidavits (if required).

Items 5, 6, 7 - Attach three copies of the DD Form 1056.  If visa photos are required, affix to back of the last copy of the DD Form 1056. *Retain a copy of the DD Form 1056 for suspense control.*

*Place one staple in the upper left corner of the total application packet to secure all document.*

*NOTE:  Place expedite justification memorandum (if required) at the top of the packet.*

Figure C2.F2. <u>INCOMING DISTRIBUTION (PASSPORT and/or VISA APPLICATIONS)</u>

<u>ARMY</u>
Visa Only Including Alien
and SOFA Stamp
(Existing Passports)
_____

DIRECTOR
USASCAF
ATTN: JDHQ-TP (OPR-RM 1B870)
6604 ARMY PENTAGON
WASHINGTON, D.C., 20310-6604

Passport Only Applications
_____

PASSPORT SERVICES DoS
ATTN: ARMY LIAISON (Suite 350)
1111 19TH ST. NW
WASHINGTON, D.C. 20036-3603

<u>NAVY</u>
Visa Only Including Alien
and SOFA Stamp
(Existing Passports)
_____

DIRECTOR
USASCAF
ATTN: JDHQ-TP (OPR-RM 1B870)
6604 ARMY PENTAGON
WASHINGTON, D.C., 20310-6604

Passport Only Applications
_____

PASSPORT SERVICES DoS
ATTN: ARMY LIAISON (Suite 350)
1111 19TH ST. NW
WASHINGTON, D.C., 20036-3603

<u>AIR FORCE</u>
All Applications (Except AMC and
Family Member not requiring Visas)
_____

HQ USAF/DPLP
AF LIAISON (RM 1B874)
1550 AIR FORCE PENTAGON
WASHINGTON, D.C., 20330-1550

<u>MARINES</u>
All Applications
_____

COMMANDANT OF THE MARINE CORPS
CODE MMOS-5
HEADQUARTERS, U.S. MARINE CORPS
WASHINGTON, D.C., 20380-1775

C2.1.2.2.1. All no-fee (blue and/or green) passport applications must be processed at the Washington Regional Passport Agency. Passport agents must forward all passport applications to the addresses indicated above. The only exception is the DoS agency in Honolulu. The Honolulu Region consists of American Samoa, the Federated States of Micronesia, Guam, Hawaii, and the Northern Mariana Islands (Saipan, Rota, and Tinian). Passport agents must verify with the DoS Regional Agency in their area whether dependent passports can be processed on a case by case situation based on an emergency.

C2.1.2.2.2. Official and diplomatic passports are processed only by the Washington Regional Passport Agency.

C2.1.2.3. No-fee passports and visas for travel in conjunction with routine operations and/or missions are processed as follows:

C2.1.2.3.1. Check the FCG before completing item 11, DD Form 1056. DoD/DoS will issue passports only for those countries listed in the FCG as having a passport requirement. Commander should project travel requirements as far in advance as possible to allow personnel sufficient time (4 weeks minimum) to obtain passports using routine processing procedures. Extra time must be allocated if visa(s) are required.

C2.1.2.3.2. For actual travel requirements with no firm itinerary, departure date or for units with missions that involve unscheduled travel to several destinations (such as Explosive Ordnance Detachments), item 11, DD Form 1056 must list the country and/or countries in their area of responsibility where the FCG requires a passport or visa. Item 12, DD Form 1056 must be left blank. Include a projected date of travel in item 14. Indicate in item 17, DD Form 1056, whether a visa is or is not required at the time of application.

C2.1.2.4. Passport Processing for Group and/or Unit Movements. Generally, passports and/or visas are not required for group and/or unit movements. In the event a requirement exists, a project officer should be appointed. The project officer will not be a passport agent, but may be a DD Form 1056 authorizing official. The project officer must contact USASCAF, DSN 227-9221, commercial (703) 697-9221, or appropriate OPR immediately for instructions on processing the group and/or unit's passport and/or visa applications.

C2.1.2.5. Passport Processing for Foreign Area Officers (EAO), Personnel Exchange Programs (PEP) and Cadet Troop Leadership Training Programs (CTLT). Use the same procedures for completion of the DD Form 1056, except as follows:

C2.1.2.5.1. Official travel or PCS orders must accompany each application. Orders must show a no-fee passport is necessary, listing the name of each destination requiring a passport and/or visa. (These countries must also be listed in item 11, DD Form 1056.) If not listed on the applicant's orders, consult with the applicant for other documentation that will provide a listing of countries. Correspondence from the sponsor or Defense Attach Office (DAO) is acceptable to augment orders that do not have the specific destinations listed.

C2.1.2.5.2. Item 14, DD Form 1056, must indicate the date the applicant will depart for PCS/TDY/TAD.

C2.1.2.5.3. Item 17, DD Form 1056, must indicate "Visas Not Required" or "Visas Required." Whether or not to include the name of the applicant's program; e.g., FAO, PEP, CTLT, etc., is optional.

C2.1.2.5.4. Family members are entitled to passports and/or visa required for PCS assignments. Family members are not authorized to receive official passports based upon their projected travel requirements (while accompanying their sponsor), unless documentation is presented showing that the family member will utilize Government transportation or be paid per diem while traveling.

C2.1.3. <u>Where to Apply for a Passport</u>

C2.1.3.1. In the United States, DoD personnel and family members apply through installation and/or activity passport agents.

C2.1.3.2. When no passport agent is available, passports may be applied for or information obtained from:

C2.1.3.2.1. Clerk of a Federal or State Court authorized by law.

C2.1.3.2.2. Certain designated Post Office Clerks.

C2.1.3.2.3. DoS Passport Agencies. The locations of the DoS Regional Passport Agencies are provided in the DoS Passport Agent's Manual (reference (b)). If not available, information can be obtained from the Post Office, USASCAF or appropriate OPR.

C2.1.3.2.4. A special postage service fee and an execution of application fee can be charged for each application made to a passport agent not on a military installation and/or activity.

C2.1.3.2.5. Outside the United States, applicants should request instructions from their personnel office or the nearest U.S. Embassy or Consular Post.

C2.1.4. <u>Identification of Applicant</u>. Applicants must establish their identity to the satisfaction of the passport agent. Chapter 1., subsection C1.4.10., outlines documents required for the proper identification of DoD personnel. Establishing the identity of the applicant and recording this information on the application form is the most important function of the passport agent.

C2.1.5. <u>Evidence of Citizenship</u>

C2.1.5.1. Applicants must submit proper evidence of U.S. citizenship with each passport application.

C2.1.5.1.1. A previously issued U.S. passport is the primary means for satisfying this requirement. Applicants born in the United States who cannot submit a passport, may submit a certified copy of their birth certificate, issued under the seal of the official custodian of their birth records, as a primary proof of citizenship. Birth certificates must have the date the certificate was filed in the registrar's office to be acceptable proof.

C2.1.5.1.2. A person born abroad, who claims U.S. citizenship at birth may submit his or her Certificate of Citizenship issued by the INS.

C2.1.5.1.3. Refer to Chapter 3, DoS Passport Agent's Manual (reference (b)) for specific information on the types of documentation that are acceptable to verify citizenship.

C2.1.5.2. For readiness reasons, DoD civilian and Armed Forces personnel should keep acceptable evidence of U.S. citizenship (certified copy of birth certificate with raised seal or previously issued passport) on hand to enable them to apply for passports on short notice. Obtaining certified copies of documents from the official custodian of records can be a time-consuming process, especially if residing in an overseas location.

C2.1.6. Passport Photographs. Submit two recent identical photographs (within 6 months) with each passport application. Visa requests may require additional photos. Photographs are accepted only at the time of application. Passport photos may be color or black and white, taken in normal street attire, without a hat or dark lens glasses. Uniforms, work clothing, T-shirts, and multicolored sports shirts are unacceptable. The servicing or most convenient military photo lab provides photo service for no-fee passports. See Chapter 5 of reference (b) for additional requirements.

C2.1.7. Assembly of Passport and/or Visa Applications DD Form 1056 and Related Documents). Applications must be assembled consistently to avoid delays. Assemble in the order listed in paragraph C2.1.7.1., below, and secure by one staple in the upper left comer of DSP Form 11/DSP Form 82 or DSP Form 19. Do not use paper clips as they will not keep the packet together during shipping and handling. Attention to detail will avoid applications from being returned for discrepancies. Refer to figure C2.F1. for the content and proper assembly of applications. From top to bottom, the assembly sequence for an application is as follows:

C2.1.7.1. Within the United States forward application in accordance with Figure C2.F2.

C2.1.7.1.1.  DSP Form 11 (Passport Application) with photo stapled to designated spot with four staples (one vertically in each comer, do not damage facial features).

C2.1.7.1.2.  Second photo directly behind DSP Form 11.  This photo should be placed facing forward, upside down.  This is the photo that will be affixed to the passport.  Be careful not to damage facial features.

C2.1.7.1.3.  If the application is for a diplomatic passport, a copy of the sponsor's PCS orders or written assignment intent, instructions, or message must be included.

C2.1.7.1.4.  Citizenship evidence (e.g., previously issued passport or other acceptable birth and/or citizenship evidence) opened, so it can be easily read.

C2.1.7.1.5.  See Figure C2.F1. for assembly procedures.

C2.1.7.2.  Outside the United States, the passport agent and/or military courier will follow the assembly procedures issued by the servicing U.S. Embassy or Consulate.

## C2.2.  APPLYING FOR A VISA

C2.2.1.  Visa, Application Requirements.  Requirements and processing time vary for each country.  They may vary within a country according to whether travel is for official, diplomatic, or personal reasons, and length of stay.  Use the FCG (reference (c)) to determine visa requirements, number of photos needed, and any additional documentation.  Reference (c) is updated and published quarterly.  It is the most accurate resource book available for guidance.

C2.2.1.1.  Within the United States, USASCAF or the appropriate OPR obtains visas for official travel and stocks most visa application forms.  Questions on visas for official travel may be referred to USASCAF, RM. 1B872, ATTN:  JDHQ-TP (Visa Section), Washington, DC  20310-3111; DSN 225-7100; Commercial (703) 695-7100.

C2.2.1.2.  Outside the United States, applicants will comply with instructions from both U.S. and foreign Embassies or Consulates, as necessary.

C2.2.2.  Visa Application Procedures

CHAPTER 2

C2.2.2.1. Within the United States, OPRs will obtain the required visas for no-fee passports after DoS Passport Services issues the no-fee passport.

C2.2.2.1.1. If an applicant requires a no-fee passport and visa, assemble the visa documents as shown in item 4, Figure C2.F1. Attach photographs to a copy of DD Form 1056 as shown in item 5, and mail the assembled passport applications as shown in Figure C2.F2. Visas are obtained based on information provided on DD Form 1056. Passport agents must allow for mail delays or express mail to ensure overnight arrival.

C2.2.2.1.2. If an applicant has a no-fee passport with 6 months validity remaining (after departure date), and requires only the issuance of visas, passport agents will attach the passport with visa documents and photographs to a copy of the DD Form 1056, and mail them along with the original and one copy of the DD Form 1056.

C2.2.2.1.3. A group of 19 or more passports requiring the same visa action must be accompanied by a letter of transmittal listing the names and destinations, including itinerary, of the group (transmittals speed up processing time).

C2.2.2.1.4. Passports will be returned with visas to the address indicated on DD Form 1056, item 13.

C2.2.2.1.5. For planning purposes, allow 30 days for visa processing. If both a passport and visa are required the total processing time may run 60 days. Multiple visas may require additional time.

C2.2.2.2. Outside the United States, applicants shall follow instructions from their Major or Combatant Commands and Embassies or Consulates.

C2.2.3. Visa Denials

C2.2.3.1. If a host country denies a visa to any DoD personnel or family member because of exclusionary policies, or for reasons other than qualifications or ability, take the following actions:

C2.2.3.1.1. Within the United States, OPRs will notify the Office of the Under Secretary of Defense for Policy (OUSD)(P).

CHAPTER 2

C2.2.3.1.2. Outside the United States, the organization that processes the visa request will send a message directly to the OUSD(P).

C2.2.3.2. Address OUSD(P) messages to report the denial of visas to: "SECDEF WASH DC/IUSDP:ADMIN." Use the following message format for:

C2.2.3.2.1. DoD personnel:

C2.2.3.2.1.1. Applicant's full name, grade, and social security number.

C2.2.3.2.1.2. Applicant's present assignment and location.

C2.2.3.2.1.3. Country that denied visa.

C2.2.3.2.1.4. Date of visa denial.

C2.2.3.2.1.5. Date of visa application.

C2.2.3.2.1.6. Reason for visa denial, if known. Report the basis of denial if the denial is based on an exclusionary policy.

C2.2.3.2.2. Family members:

C2.2.3.2.2.1. Applicant's full name and relationship to sponsor.

C2.2.3.2.2.2. Sponsor's full name, grade, and social security number.

C2.2.3.2.2.3. Present assignment and location of sponsor.

C2.2.3.2.2.4. Present location of family member.

C2.2.3.2.2.5. Country that denied visa.

C2.2.3.2.2.6. Date of travel approval (state whether approved travel is concurrent or nonconcurrent).

C2.2.3.2.2.7. Date of visa application.

C2.2.3.2.2.8. Date of visa denial.

C2.2.3.2.2.9. Reason for visa denial, if known. Report the basis of the denial if the denial is biased on an exclusionary policy.

C2.2.3.3. When completed, the message will be "FOR OFFICLAL USE ONLY."

## C2.3. COMPLETION OF DD FORM 1056, "AUTHORIZATION TO APPLY FOR A NO-FEE PASSPORT AND/OR REQUEST FOR VISA"

C2.3.1. DD Form 1056 certifies applicants are on authorized travel and entitled to no-fee passports. It is the authority for the DoS to issue no-fee passports. DD Form 1056 is required for each application. The same DD Form 1056 is used to request visas. DD Form 1056 is also submitted with no-fee passports requiring amendments, corrections, extensions or additional visa pages.

C2.3.2. The following personnel are not authorized to travel on no-fee passports and therefore are not eligible to be issued DD Form 1056:

C2.3.2.1. Retired DoD employees, and their family members, traveling to foreign countries to take up residence, even if Government transportation is authorized. The only exception is if retired personnel are family members of other DoD personnel traveling on official change of station orders. In this case, DD Form 1056 may be issued if travel authorizes the retired member to accompany their sponsor.

C2.3.2.2. DoD employees, and/or family members, traveling for personal reasons, such as vacation or leave, or any reason not considered official travel.

C2.3.2.3. Civilian contract employees.

C2.3.2.4. Employees of Government Agencies and Bureaus other than the Department of Defense.

C2.3.3. Instructions for Completing DD Form 1056 (See Figures C2.F3. and C2.F4.)

C2.3.3.1. The authorizing official completes DD Form 1056 using the following guidelines before processing the application for no-fee passports and visas: (Failure to properly complete the forms will result in processing delays and/or the rejection of the application.)

C2.3.3.1.1  Type all entries except for item 16.

C2.3.3.1.2.  Enter all dates with the month typed as a three letter abbreviation, DD/MMM/YR (e.g., 1 JUN 95).

C2.3.3.1.3.  Item 1.  Enter the date.  The date in item 1 should be 10 working days before the date of departure in item 14.

C2.3.3.1.4.  Item 2.  Enter the DoD Component sponsoring the travel. (For example:  Army, Air Force, Office of the Secretary of Defense (OSD), Chairman of the Joint Chiefs of Staff, or other applicable DoD Component.)

C2.3.3.1.5.  Item 3.  Enter the applicant's full name (Last, First, and Middle) and relationship to sponsor, if applicant is a family member.  When initiating applications for more than one family member, forms should be numbered as 1 of 3, 2 of 3, etc., so that they can be processed together.

C2.3.3.1.6.  Item 4.  Enter the applicant's date of birth using the format DD/MMM/YR (e.g., 1 Jun 95).

C2.3.3.1.7.  Item 5.  If born in the United States or the U.S. territories (e.g., Guam, U.S. Virgin Islands, Puerto Rico, etc.), enter the State or territory in which born.  If born outside the United States or the U.S. territories, enter the country of birth.

C2.3.3.1.8.  Item 6.  Complete if the applicant is a family member accompanying DoD personnel (referred to as sponsor), otherwise check block.

C2.3.3.1.9.  Item 7.  Enter the civilian grade or military rank and grade. If the applicant is a family member, enter sponsor's grade or rank; e.g., CPT/O-3, SSG/E-6, GS-11.

C2.3.3.1.10.  Item 8.  Enter sponsor's social security number.

C2.3.3.1.11.  Item 9.  Enter applicant's complete current home address, area code, and telephone number.

C2.3.3.1.12.  Item 10.  Enter an interim address where applicant may be contacted after departing their permanent duty station.  Indicate leave/TDY/TAD and, if possible, include dates.  Also, include the passport agent's identification code.

C2.3.3.1.13.  Item 11.   Enter the name of the country or countries applicant is traveling to (do not list regions).   List countries in the sequence of travel and include stopover countries where passport and visas are required.   Do not use mailing addresses or names of installations or cities unless required by the FCG (reference (c)).

C2.3.3.1.14.  Item 12.   Enter the name of the special assignment, or "not applicable."   Do not list the type of passport to be issued.   Based on the assignment identified in this block, the DoS will determine what type of passport will be issued.

C2.3.3.1.14.1.  If the assignment is to Attaché, Military Assistance Advisory Group, Security Assistance Liaison, or other special advisory group or assignment that will govern type and need for a passport, enter that information.

C2.3.3.1.14.2.  If the position to be occupied is the Chief or Deputy Chief of the Special Assignment Activity, enter this information.   Also, include the name of the incumbent (if known), and give the date the assignment is expected to end.   For family members, enter information on sponsors assignment as above.

C2.3.3.1.15.  Item 13.   Enter the military address of the installation passport office or central port call office.   Include commercial and Defense Switched Network (DSN) telephone numbers from which the passport will be controlled and issued.   Building, room numbers, and phone numbers are necessary if the application requires express mail delivery to meet the travel date.   Post office box addresses are not acceptable.   When DD Form 1056 is issued overseas for family members located in the United States, enter the installation passport agent or central port call office responsible for arranging unaccompanied travel.   The address shown must be clear and complete.

C2.3.3.1.16.  Item 14.   This date is critical for DoS processing.   Enter the confirmed port call/TDY date.   If this date changes, immediately submit an updated DD Form 1056 to reflect the new dates.

C2.3.3.1.17.  Item 15.   Enter proposed length of stay.   Visa and passport requirements vary with the length of stay in some countries, as do visa lengths, which may prevent early application.

C2.3.3.1.18.  Item 16.   Enter the complete address, including office symbol, city, and State of the authorizing official.   Commercial, and DSN telephone numbers must be shown.   The signature and date of the authorizing official is mandatory. The first copy of the DD Form 1056 must contain an original signature of the authorizing official.

C2.3.3.1.19. Item 17. Used for special remarks or instructions. Indicate whether VISA REQUIRED or VISA NOT REQUIRED. Overseas agents and/or military couriers, indicate the U.S. Embassy or Consulate serving your installation, address as follows: POUCH-FRANKFURT, POUCH SEOUL, etc. If additional space is required, enter "see continuation sheets" and type the remaining information in the remarks section.

C2.3.3.2. Suspense Control. Record suspense data in items 18 through 29 of DD Form 1056. This data enables passport agents, USASCAF or appropriate OPR to track applications.

C2.3.3.2.1. Upon receipt of passport, record the passport number, date of issue, and expiration date in items 22 through 29.

C2.3.3.2.2. Applicants sign or initial in the remarks section (item 22) as receiving the passports. If mailed, enter type of mail and date mailed.

C2.3.3.2.3. When sending a valid passport for "VISA ONLY" complete items 22 through 29. This information is found inside the passport's front cover.

C2.3.3.2.4. List all documents mailed with the application in the remarks section (item 30); e.g., DSP Form 11, DSP Form 82, DSP Form 19, previous passport, certified birth certificate, etc.

C2.3.3.2.5. Copies of DD Form 1056 will be mailed and/or maintained as follows:

C2.3.3.2.5.1. Mail original and three copies with the application packet.

C2.3.3.2.5.2. Retain a copy in suspense to be used as a tracking document until the passport is received.

## C2.4. PROCESSING PASSPORT AND/OR VISA APPLICATIONS

C2.4.1. There are three types of service provided by DoS for processing official, diplomatic or any no-fee passport application requiring a visa. The DoS determines which service an application requires. If passport agents send no-fee applications, not requiring visas, to any of the other 13 DoS Regional Passport Agencies, they should verify that the office will accept no-fee passport applications and check for any unique procedures that should be followed.

C2.4.1.1. Routine. Application are considered routine if received and data entered by the DoS more than 30 workdays before the estimated date of departure without special circumstances; e.g., multiple visas. Based on the large volume of applications received at DoS, data entry may require 2 to 4 working days. Passport agents must allow for mail delivery time if express mail is not used.

C2.4.1.1.1. Normal processing for no-fee passports are 30 workdays, 45 days with a visa, and 60 days for multiple visas at the time they are data entered into the DoS system.

C2.4.1.1.2. DoD personnel normally receive PCS assignment notification in sufficient time to allow for routine passport processing. These passport applications generally will not receive expeditious processing.

C2.4.1.2. Expedite. Travel required in less than 30 workdays or special circumstances exist with regard to visas required.

C2.4.1.2.1. Passport applications requiring less than 30 workdays processing time plus postal delivery time must be accompanied by a memorandum of justification signed by a general officer or SES equivalent. The only exceptions are for applications initiated where no general officer or equivalent exists. In these cases, applications may be signed by the installation commander.

C2.4.1.2.1.1. The memorandum for expeditious processing must contain an original signature, identify the originating agency, and provide the agency's mailing address. It must also clearly state that a general officer or SES equivalent is not assigned and/or available because of leave and/or TDY. Forward expedite requests to addresses indicated at Figure C2.F2.

C2.4.1.2.1.2. Requests must be dated and contain the following information: traveler's last name, first name and middle initial, date of birth, commercial telephone number with the area code of the travel approving official signing the correspondence, date traveler was tasked for the Temporary Duty Tour (TDY) or PCS, why it is imperative that the applicant travel on the date indicated, justification for late submission, and the date required.

C2.4.1.2.2.  Applications requiring expeditious processing should be express mailed to maximize processing time.

C2.4.1.3.  <u>Walk-through</u>.   For applicants directed to travel within time-frames that make it impossible for expedited procedures to be used, walk-through service is available.   Walk-through processing is limited, used only to support travel justified by critical, emergency circumstances.   These circumstances must be verified by the applicant's organization and a memorandum of justification prepared in accordance with subparagraph C2.4.1.2.1.1., above.   The installation and/or activity passport agent must coordinate this with USASCAF or appropriate OPR.

C2.4.2.  Visa processing is prioritized according to the estimated date of travel. Visas cannot be processed any faster than allowed by the foreign embassies.   Average processing time per visa is 5 working days.   In some instances, newly issued passports must be returned to the applicant and signed before foreign embassies will process them for visas.   This will further increase processing time.   Because foreign embassies issue the visas, expedite memorandums are unnecessary except in extremely time-sensitive and/or emergency cases.

## Figure C2.F3.   DD FORM 1056 (Service Member)

*This form must be typed. See DoD 1000.21-R for form completion instructions.*

| AUTHORIZATION TO APPLY FOR A "NO-FEE" PASSPORT AND/OR REQUEST FOR VISA | 1. DATE PASSPORT OR VISA REQUIRED BY APPLICANT<br>11 July 1996 | 2. MAJOR SERVICE COMPONENT<br>Army |
|---|---|---|
| **3. APPLICANT'S LAST NAME - FIRST NAME - MIDDLE NAME**<br>Hayes, Monica Susan | **4. APPLICANT'S DATE OF BIRTH**<br>4 June 1945 | **5. APPLICANT'S PLACE OF BIRTH**<br>Austin, Tx |
| **6. SPONSOR'S LAST NAME - FIRST NAME - MIDDLE NAME**<br>X   *(If same as Item 3, X block)* | **7. SPONSOR'S MILITARY RANK/CIVILIAN GRADE**<br>Major/O4 | **8. SPONSOR'S SSN**<br>664-33-1234 |

| 9.a. APPLICANT'S CURRENT HOME ADDRESS *(Include ZIP Code)*<br>45 Orchard Road<br>Vancouver, Wa   98665 | b. HOME TELEPHONE NUMBER *(Include area code)* |
|---|---|
| | c. OFFICE TELEPHONE NUMBER *(Include area code/DSN)* |

| 10.a. INTERIM ADDRESS WHERE APPLICANT MAY BE CONTACTED AFTER DEPARTING LOCATION INDICATED IN ITEM 9 *(Include ZIP Code)* | b. NAME OF PERSON WITH WHOM RESIDING | |
|---|---|---|
| | c. TELEPHONE *(Incl. area code)* | d. AGENT ID CODE *(If applicable)*<br>WA297 |

| 11. DESTINATION *(Country or Countries)*<br>Israel<br>Egypt | 12. SPECIAL ASSIGNMENT REQUIRING PASSPORT* *(See Note)*<br>ATMO | 13. PASSPORT WILL BE FORWARDED TO: *(Include complete mailing address, building number, room number, ZIP Code, and telephone number/DSN)*<br>Transportation Office<br>Bldg 5162, ATTN: AFZH-AGI-GP<br>Ft Lewis, Wa  98433-5000<br>(907) 298-1471 DSN: 397-5829 |
|---|---|---|
| **14. ESTIMATED DATE OF DEPARTURE** *(From country in which applicant is currently residing)*<br>25 July 1996 | **15. PROPOSED LENGTH OF STAY**<br>30 days | **16. AUTHORIZING OFFICIAL**<br>a. NAME *(Last, First, Middle Initial)*<br>Jones, Barbara L. |
| **17. ADDITIONAL INFORMATION** *(Attach continuation sheets if necessary)*<br><br>(State whether a visa is required or not.  If required, visa info must be listed.) | | b. GRADE<br>GS-13  c. TITLE<br>Chief |
| | | d. COMPLETE MAILING ADDRESS *(Include ZIP Code)*<br>Transportation Office<br>ATTN: SATQ-P<br>Ft Lewis, Wa  98433-5000 |
| | | e. TELEPHONE NUMBER *(Include area code/DSN)* |
| | | f. SIGNATURE OF AUTHORIZING OFFICIAL   g. DATE<br>1 Jun 96 |

| FOR USE BY ISSUING OR RECEIVING AGENT *(Suspense Control)* | | |
|---|---|---|
| **18. DATE APPLIED FOR PASSPORT**<br>1 June 1996 | **19. PLACE APPLIED FOR PASSPORT**<br>Ft Lewis, Wa | **20. NAME OF COURT OR PASSPORT AGENT**<br>Ms. Johnson |
| **21. DATE PASSPORT RECEIVED FROM DEPARTMENT OF STATE**<br>20 July 1996 | **22. PASSPORT NUMBER** | **23. DATE OF PASSPORT ISSUE** / **24. PASSPORT EXPIRATION DATE** |
| **25. DOCUMENT(S) INCLUDED WITH PASSPORT**<br>Birth Certificate | **26. COUNTRY AND DATE VISA REQUESTED** | **27. DATE PASSPORT RECEIVED WITH VISA** / **28. DATE PASSPORT MAILED** |

**PRIVACY ACT STATEMENT**

AUTHORITY: Sections 3012, 8012, 5031, Title 10 USC; 22 CFR 51.63; EO 9397.

PRINCIPAL PURPOSE: To provide authority for issue of "No-Fee" passport and/or request for a visa which is an endorsement stamped or written on a passport, showing that it has been examined by the proper officials of a country and granting entry into that country. The Social Security Number is required to verify and/or identify the applicant.

ROUTINE USES: Information is used in conjunction with application for passport/visa and foreign travel.  Information may be released to other DoD agencies, various activities within the Department of State, foreign embassies and consulates.

DISCLOSURE: Voluntary; however, if applicant does not provide information, a "No-Fee" passport cannot be authorized.

*NOTE: If assignment is to Attache; MAAG; JUSMMAT; Security Assistance Liaison Office (SALO); OSP or other Special Advisory Group, e.g., CENTO; or any particular assignment that will govern type and need for a passport, enter such information. If not, enter "Not Applicable."

DD FORM 1056, MAY 96           PREVIOUS EDITION MAY BE USED.

## Figure C2.F4.   DD FORM 1056 (Family Member)

*This form must be typed. See DoD 1000.21-R for form completion instructions.*

| | | |
|---|---|---|
| **AUTHORIZATION TO APPLY FOR A "NO-FEE" PASSPORT AND/OR REQUEST FOR VISA** | **1. DATE PASSPORT OR VISA REQUIRED BY APPLICANT** <br> 11 July 1996 | **2. MAJOR SERVICE COMPONENT** <br> U.S. Army |
| **3. APPLICANT'S LAST NAME - FIRST NAME - MIDDLE NAME** <br> Browne, Mary Lousie | **4. APPLICANT'S DATE OF BIRTH** <br> 25 Dec 1972 | **5. APPLICANT'S PLACE OF BIRTH** <br> Baltimore, Md |
| **6. SPONSOR'S LAST NAME - FIRST NAME - MIDDLE NAME** <br> Browne, Larry James <br> (If same as Item 3, X block) | **7. SPONSOR'S MILITARY RANK/CIVILIAN GRADE** <br> GS-12 | **8. SPONSOR'S SSN** <br> 015-00-0011 |

**9.a. APPLICANT'S CURRENT HOME ADDRESS** *(Include ZIP Code)*
132 McDonald Court
Universal City, Tx   78154

**b. HOME TELEPHONE NUMBER** *(Include area code)*
301-372-1222

**c. OFFICE TELEPHONE NUMBER** *(Include area code/DSN)*
703-625-2522

**10.a. INTERIM ADDRESS WHERE APPLICANT MAY BE CONTACTED AFTER DEPARTING LOCATION INDICATED IN ITEM 9** *(Include ZIP Code)*

**b. NAME OF PERSON WITH WHOM RESIDING**

**c. TELEPHONE** *(Incl. area code)*

**d. AGENT ID CODE** *(If applicable)*
TH297

**11. DESTINATION** *(Country or Countries)*
Germany

**12. SPECIAL ASSIGNMENT REQUIRING PASSPORT*** *(See Note)*
NA

**13. PASSPORT WILL BE FORWARDED TO:** *(Include complete mailing address, building number, room number, ZIP Code, and telephone number/DSN)*
Transportation Office
Bldg 247, ATTN: TA20-AGB-TP
Ft Sam Houston, Tx  88231-5000
(BTS) 221-0728 / DSN: 972-0590

**14. ESTIMATED DATE OF DEPARTURE** *(From country in which applicant is currently residing)*
25 July 1996

**15. PROPOSED LENGTH OF STAY**
Two years

**16. AUTHORIZING OFFICIAL**

**a. NAME** *(Last, First, Middle Initial)*
Brothers, Rosa L.

**b. GRADE** GS-13 | **c. TITLE** Director

**d. COMPLETE MAILING ADDRESS** *(Include ZIP Code)*
Travel Assistance
ATTN:  TAOF-P
Ft Sam Houston, Tx  88234-5000

**e. TELEPHONE NUMBER** *(Include area code/DSN)*

**17. ADDITIONAL INFORMATION** *(Attach continuation sheets if necessary)*

(Additional visas, assignment information, etc.)

**f. SIGNATURE OF AUTHORIZING OFFICIAL**

**g. DATE**
30 May 1996

---

**FOR USE BY ISSUING OR RECEIVING AGENT** *(Suspense Control)*

| **18. DATE APPLIED FOR PASSPORT** <br> 1 June 1996 | **19. PLACE APPLIED FOR PASSPORT** | **20. NAME OF COURT OR PASSPORT AGENT** <br> Ms. Smith | |
|---|---|---|---|
| **21. DATE PASSPORT RECEIVED FROM DEPARTMENT OF STATE** <br> 20 July 1996 | **22. PASSPORT NUMBER** | **23. DATE OF PASSPORT ISSUE** | **24. PASSPORT EXPIRATION DATE** |
| **25. DOCUMENT(S) INCLUDED WITH PASSPORT** | **26. COUNTRY AND DATE VISA REQUESTED** | **27. DATE PASSPORT RECEIVED WITH VISA** | **28. DATE PASSPORT MAILED** |

---

**PRIVACY ACT STATEMENT**

**AUTHORITY:** Sections 3012, 8012, 5031, Title 10 USC; 22 CFR 51.63; EO 9397.

**PRINCIPAL PURPOSE:** To provide authority for issue of "No-Fee" passport and/or request for a visa which is an endorsement stamped or written on a passport, showing that it has been examined by the proper officials of a country and granting entry into that country. The Social Security Number is required to verify and/or identify the applicant.

**ROUTINE USES:** Information is used in conjunction with application for passport/visa and foreign travel. Information may be released to other DoD agencies, various activities within the Department of State, foreign embassies and consulates.

**CLOSURE:** Voluntary; however, if applicant does not provide information, a "No-Fee" passport cannot be authorized.

NOTE: If assignment is to Attache; MAAG; JUSMMAT; Security Assistance Liaison Office (SALO); OSP or other Special Advisory Group, e.g., CENTO; or any particular assignment that will govern type and need for a passport, enter such information. If not, enter "Not Applicable."

**DD FORM 1056, MAY 95**          PREVIOUS EDITION MAY BE USED.

## C3. CHAPTER 3

## PASSPORT AGENT NOMINATION AND DESIGNATION PROCEDURES

### C3.1. PASSPORT AGENT NOMINATIONS

The DoD Executive Agent for Passport and Passport Agent Services has authority to approve nominations of DoD civilian and military personnel to serve as passport agents at military installations and/or activities. The following applies to candidates nominated as passport agents:

C3.1.1. Nominees must be U.S. citizens.

C3.1.2. Nominees must be available to serve at least 1 year.

C3.1.3. Nominees must be in the pay grade E-4 or above for military personnel or GS-4 or above for civilian personnel.

### C3.2. PASSPORT AGENT DESIGNATION PROCEDURES

C3.2.1. Outside the United States. Personnel under the UCMJ Article 136 (reference (h)), 10 U.S.C. 936 (reference (i)), 5 U.S. C. 2903 (reference j)), and those designated as passport agents and/or military couriers by the commander will accept and process passport applications as instructed by the commander of a Major or Combatant Command.

C3.2.2. Within the United States

C3.2.2.1. The Executive Agent has redelegated to the Military Departments the authority to approve or disapprove their own passport agent appointments. When forwarding agent designation memorandums, the Military Departments will use the authority line "For the DoD Executive Agent."

C3.2.2.2. Nomination format is at Figure C3.F1. All required information must be completed. Both the nominee and authorizing official must sign the memorandum. Each nomination will include verification of U.S. citizenship. The original and three copies must be forwarded through the Service OPR to the DoD Executive Agent. Addresses are at Figure C3.F2. A copy of the approved agent nomination must be maintained by the authorizing official.

## Figure C3.F1.   SAMPLE AGENT APPOINTMENT/CANCELLATION REQUEST

---

**(SAMPLE AGENT APPOINTMENT/CANCELLATION REQUEST)**

---

**(USE "DoD  COMPONENT" CORRESPONDENCE FORMAT)**

**(SEE ADDRESS LISTING AT Figure 3-2)**

SUBJECT:   Appointment/Cancellation of Passport Agent

1.  Request appointment of below listed individual (s) as  passport agent (s).  The following information is provided in accordance with DoD Regulation 1000.21-R.

      a.  Full Name:_____Grade/Rank:_____Birthplace:_____

      b.  DSN, Commercial, and FAX Numbers:_____

      c.  E-Mail Address: _____

      d.  Message Address:

_____

      d.  Organization Mailing Address:  (Include unit designation, office symbol, street address, building number, room number and zip+four)._____

      e.  Number of Passports Processed Each Month:_____

      f.  Agent Being Replaced:  (Full name, grade/rank and agent ID code)_____

2.  Justification:  (Justification is only required if this is a new request or requesting additional agents)._____

3.  Please contact  (Name, grade/rank at DSN/commercial numbers _____ ) if you have any questions.


**(Signature of agent nominee)**
(name and grade)

**(Signature of Authorizing Official)**
(name, grade and title)

1st Ind:  (DoD approval office)

Your request is approved/disapproved.  Agent is assigned agent ID code _____.


_____
DoD Approval/Disapproval Authority

## Figure C3.F2.   MILITARY OPRs

### MILITARY OPRs

#### ARMY

USASCAF
ATTN: JDHQ-TP (OPR-RM 1B874)
6604 ARMY PENTAGON
WASHINGTON, D.C 20310-6604

#### AIR FORCE

HQ USAF/DPLP
ATTN:  AF LIAISON (RM 1B874)
1550 AF PENTAGON
WASHINGTON, D.C.  20330-1550

#### NAVY

CHIEF OF NAVAL PERSONNEL (PERS 3)
2 NAVY ANNEX
WASHINGTON, D.C. 20370-3310

#### MARINES

COMMANDANT OF THE MARINE CORPS
CODE MMOS-5
HEADQUARTERS, U.S. MARINE CORPS
WASHINGTON, D.C.  20380-1775

## C3.3.   REGULAR-FEE PASSPORT APPLICATIONS

Passport agents will decline to accept applications for regular-fee passports except in unusual circumstances and only after written approval by the DoD Executive Agent and DoS.   Exceptions will be forwarded through the Service OPR to the DoD Executive Agent.   Include the following information:

C3.3.1.  Passport agent's name and location.

C3.3.2.  The number of regular-fee applications the passport agent wishes to accept.

C3.3.3.  Justification for the request.

C3.3.4.  The nearest passport agent authorized to accept regular-fee passport applications.

CHAPTER 3

## C4. CHAPTER 4

## QUALITY CONTROL, DISTRIBUTION, AND DISPOSITION

### C4.1. QUALITY CHECKS

C4.1.1. Passport and Visa Applications. To prevent processing delays, passport agents must ensure all requirements are met. Passport agents shall carefully screen each application, once assembled, to provide a quality check. The DoS/OPR shall notify passport agents of incomplete or incorrect applications. Applications are held in the DoS/OPR suspense for 30 days pending the receipt of missing or corrected documents. Failure to respond by the suspense date results in suspended applications being canceled by the DoS. Once canceled, the agent must resubmit a new application. Following the DoS and the DoD guidelines, along with attention to detail, will help avoid delays.

C4.1.2. Correction or Amendment of Passports

C4.1.2.1. Within the United States, return no-fee passports containing errors or omissions as soon as possible or within 30 days after issuance, in accordance with paragraph C4.3., (Distribution), with original and three copies of DD Form 1056, and a Passport Amendment and/or Validation Application (DSP Form 19). Show correction desired in item 17, DD Form 1056, and the DSP Form 19 and forward all supporting documents required to verify corrections: e.g., birth certificate if the birth date is incorrect. It takes 20 to 30 days to receive corrected passports.

C4.1.2.2. In overseas areas, follow instructions from Commanders of Major or Combatant Commands and send the passport to one of the following offices:

C4.1.2.2.1. The servicing Passport Service Center or Office, (which will forward it to the U.S. Consulate Office or Embassy), or directly to:

C4.1.2.2.2. The U.S. Consulate Office or Embassy.

### C4.2. CONTROL

C4.2.1. The No-Fee Passport as Government Property

C4.2.1.1. A U.S. no-fee passport is an official document of the U.S. Government and remains at all times-the property of the U.S. Government. A no-fee passport shall be surrendered to an authorized representative of the U.S. Government upon demand.   Authorized representatives of the U.S. Government are authorized to confiscate official no-fee passports upon notice of stop movement actions.

C4.2.1.2.  Passports shall not be altered, mutilated, or changed in any manner, except as authorized and changed by DoS Passport Services, its agencies, or by a consular post abroad upon proper authorization from DoS Passport Services.   Anyone who mutilates or makes an unauthorized change of a passport is subject to criminal penalties (18 U.S.C. 1543 reference (e)).

C4.2.2.  Safeguarding No-Fee Passports.   Commanders shall ensure that no-fee passports issued to persons within their command are kept current and safeguarded as follows:

C4.2.2.1.  Personnel in overseas areas with duty requiring passports shall be checked periodically to ensure their passports are in order.   Applications for renewal shall be submitted when passports have not more than 12 months and not less than 7 months validity remaining.   Personnel must not be within 6 months of their date of eligibility to return from overseas.

C4.2.2.2.  When DoD personnel and their family members complete travel abroad and return to the United States, passports shall be turned into the gaining installation or activity for safekeeping.   The appropriate office handling travel arrangements shall establish procedures to ensure that personnel returning from overseas areas are counseled concerning this obligation.   Installations and/or activities are authorized to retain passports for future official travel.   Personnel being separated and/or discharged from the overseas command and immediately returning to the United States are authorized to retain their passports for future proof of citizenship.   DoD personnel and family members must be counseled that an official passport may not be used for personal travel.

C4.2.2.3.  If travel is canceled, the installation and/or activity shall safeguard the passport until the individual departs on PCS and/or TDY or until the passport expires.   Expired no-fee passports must be canceled in accordance with subsection C4.4.5. of this chapter.

C4.2.2.4.  When not in use, passports shall be safeguarded by installations and/or activities in a secure manner, as deemed appropriate by the commander.   As a minimum, passports and/or passport applications must be secured in a locked office when not in use by or under the direct supervision of an authorized person.   Passports and passport applications must be handled and stored under conditions adequate to prevent unauthorized persons from gaining access.

## C4.3. DISTRIBUTION

### C4.3.1. Mailing Instructions

C4.3.1.1. Passports, passport applications, and/or visa applications shall be sent first-class through the U.S. postal system, commercial (overnight) express company, or an official courier within the United States, or the U.S. territories. Passports may be mailed to an Army or Air Force Post Office or Fleet Post Office. Passports shall not be sent by international mail. In foreign countries, DoS pouch service may be used. Applications submitted within 30 workdays of the estimated departure requiring expeditious processing should be sent by express mail.

C4.3.1.2. Passport agents shall determine where to send passport applications depending upon whether the application includes visa requirements and depending upon which DoS Regional Passport Agency services their location.

C4.3.1.2.1. All applications submitted for no-fee diplomatic, official, and no-fee (blue and/or green) passports that require visas shall be mailed to the appropriate OPR or DoS, Passport Services, ATTN: ARMY LIAISON (SUITE 350), 1111 19th Street, NW, Washington, DC 20036-3603. See restrictions on international mail in subparagraph C4.3.1.1., above.

C4.3.1.2.2. All applications for no-fee (blue and/or green) passports not requiring visas shall be mailed to the DoS Regional Passport Agency within their area. Passport agents must verify that the DoS Regional Agency will accept no-fee passport applications. Refer to the DoS Passport Agent's Manual (reference (b)) for the exact address of the Regional Passport Agency within your area. If a Regional Passport Agency processes the application, all correspondence or tracer requests will be submitted between the requesting activity and that agency. Do not send information copies to OPRS.

C4.3.1.2.3. Applications for no-fee passports for employees of DoD Non-Appropriated Fund Instrumentality's and their family members shall be mailed to the DoS, PASSPORT-SERVICES, ATTN: ARMY LIAISON (SUITE 350), 1111 19th Street, NW, Washington, DC 20036-3603 for processing.

### C4.3.2. Distribution and Receipt of Passports

C4.3.2.1.  DoS Passport Agencies, USASCAF, and Military Service OPRs shall mail completed passports directly to the passport agent address in Item 13, DD Form 1056.

C4.3.2.2.  Upon receipt of completed passports and visas, agents shall inspect for accuracy and completeness.

C4.3.2.2.1.  If no discrepancies are found, passports shall be secured until the authorized time of travel.

C4.3.2.2.2.  If discrepancies are found, follow the procedures for correction or amendment of passports in Chapter 4., subsection C4.1.2.

## C4.4.  DISPOSITION

C4.4.1.  Cancellation of Travel.  Immediately notify USASCAF or appropriate OPR by message or telefax if travel is canceled after a passport application is submitted.  Provide applicant's name, sponsors name (if family members are involved), destination, date and place of passport application and a copy of the DD Form 1056.  If the passport has been received before cancellation of travel, the passport agent is responsible for maintaining the passport in a secure manner until needed.  Review passports for correctness; then file.

C4.4.2.  Procedures for Inquiring the Status of No-Fee Passports

C4.4.2.1.  When DD Form 1056 is completed, the suspense control enables passport agents to monitor applications.  When passports are received no earlier than 10 workdays before the planned departure date, and there is no known reason for a delay, the passport agent should initiate the following tracer actions:

C4.4.2.1.1.  No more than 10 workdays before planned departure date, the passport agent may request a status by sending a message to USASCAF PENTAGON WASH DC/JDHQ-TPH, telefax (DSN) 223-3730, (COM) (703) 693-3730, appropriate OPR or the DoS Regional Passport Agency.  Only USASCAF or appropriate OPR is authorized to contact DoS Passport Services, Washington, DC, or Foreign Embassies regarding the status of passports and visa applications.  Status requests should not be generated until 10 workdays before departure, because many visas cannot be processed until 30 (or fewer) days before the date of arrival in a country. Final processing, therefore, cannot be executed before the 30 (or fewer) day window.

C4.4.2.1.1.1. When initiating a tracer through message centers, all the information from items 1, 3, 4, 7, 8, 11, 12, 14, 15, and 17 of DD Form 1056 (this information must be exactly as it appears on the submitted DD Form 1056) and the name and telephone numbers (DSN and commercial) of the passport agent initiating the tracer are mandatory.

C4.4.2.1.1.2. When initiating a tracer by telefax, the passport agent shall transmit a copy of the DD Form 1056.

C4.4.2.2. No earlier than 10 workdays before departure date, passport agents should telephonically inquire the status of applications. If applications require multiple (three or more) visas, agents should wait for 15 workdays before the planned departure date before making inquiries. This applies if the applicant's signature is required by the embassy prior to issuing a visa.

C4.4.2.3. Passport agents at selected installations and/or activities possess limited access to the DoD computer database that provides them an immediate status check on all applications they have submitted for processing.

C4.4.2.4. Individual applicants are not authorized to execute tracer actions. All requests for tracers must come from the passport agent of record.

C4.4.3. <u>If a Passport is not Received Before Planned Departure Date</u>

C4.4.3.1. If it is known that a passport cannot be obtained before the applicant's departure from the losing installation, the passport agent or central port call office must:

C4.4.3.1.1. Verify address and telephone number in item 10, DD Form 1056.

C4.4.3.1.2. Ensure DoD personnel understand that if family member passports are not received before the port call date, military personnel must depart as scheduled.

C4.4.3.1.3. Advise the DoD personnel and family members that they are not to report to the Aerial Port of Embarkation without no-fee passports (and visas, if applicable). They will not be allowed to board the aircraft without a passport and visa, if required.

C4.4.3.2. If passports are not received by the passport agent by the departure date, the passport agent should contact USASCAF or appropriate OPR. Personnel should not, under normal circumstances, be allowed to outprocess and/or depart without the required passport.

C4.4.4. Lost or Stolen Passports

C4.4.4.1. Domestic Locations. See DoS Passport Agent's Manual (reference (b)).

C4.4.4.2. Overseas Areas. Contact the servicing passport center or direct inquiries to the nearest U.S. Embassy or Consulate.

C4.4.5. Cancellation of Passports

C4.4.5.1. All valid no-fee passports, when no longer needed, must be canceled. The following procedures apply: Do not cancel passports, valid or expired, when submitting for a new passport of the same type. DoS will cancel and return (if requested) passports in connection with new applications. Do not cancel a valid passport when submitted as evidence of citizenship with an application for a different type passport; e.g., (the MOA reference (k)) applicant requests issuance of a second official passport.

C4.4.5.1.1. Family member and no-fee regular passports: If the bearer of a valid no-fee regular or family member requests cancellation for reasons other than the issuance of a new passport, cancel and return to the bearer. Military personnel, DoD civilians, and family members stationed within the United States must have their passports canceled when separating from the Military and/or Government Service. Additionally, passports must be canceled when individuals are assigned to positions not requiring passports. Personnel, including family members, separating from overseas must comply with instruction issued by the overseas command.

NOTE: A DSP 19 (Passport Amendment and/or Validation Application) is not required for family member passports unless the passport is being destroyed, (see subsection C4.4.6, below).

C4.4.5.1.2. Official passports: A DSP Form 19 must be completed if the bearer of a valid official passport requests cancellation for reasons other than the issuance of new passport of the same type. Passport agents must forward the DSP 19 in accordance with the DoS Passport Agent's Manual (reference (b)).

C4.4.5.1.3. Diplomatic Passports: A DSP 19 must be completed if the bearer of a valid diplomatic passport requests cancellation for reasons other than the issuance of a new passport. Passport agents must forward the diplomatic passport along with the DSP 19 in accordance with reference (b). Indicate if the applicant desires the canceled passport returned.

C4.4.5.2. If no new passport of any type is being requested, cancel the passport (other than diplomatic) with a rubber stamp bearing the word "CANCELED" (letters should be approximately 1 inch high). If the passport is not machine-readable, place the stamp diagonally across the descriptive data page. If the passport is machine-readable, place the stamp diagonally across the secretary's message page directly opposite the data page. Invalidate the machine-readable code at the bottom of the data page by punching two holes, about one inch apart, through the coded data.

C4.4.6. Destruction of Passports. Passport agents processing unclaimed passports (attempts to locate the bearer have failed) may destroy the passports. Destruction should be accomplished by shredding and/or burning. Destruction procedures applies to family member and official passports only. Diplomatic passports must be returned to the DoS with a completed DSP Form 19.

# C5. CHAPTER 5

## REQUIRED FORMS AND PUBLICATIONS

### C5.1. REQUIRED DoD FORM

DD Form 1056 is submitted for all DoD personnel and family members applying for a no-fee passport and visas. See Chapter 2. for the proper use of this form. This Regulation prescribes Form 1056. The DoD Executive Agent is the proponent for this form.

### C5.2. REQUIRED DoS FORMS (DSP FORMS)

C5.2.1. The DoS forms listed below are authorized by the DoS Passport Agent's Manual (reference (b)) and are prescribed by this Regulation for use by all DoD Components. Military passport agents will use these forms for processing passports and passport applications. Detailed use of these forms is provided in reference (b) and on the reverse of some of the forms.

C5.2.1.1. Form DSP 10A, "Birth Affidavit"

C5.2.1.2. Form DSP 11, "Passport Application"

C5.2.1.3. Form DSP 19, "Passport Amendment/Validation Application"

C5.2.1.4. Form DSP 63, "Affidavit Regarding Change-of Name"

C5.2.1.5. Form DSP 64, "Statement Regarding Lost or Stolen Passport"

C5.2.1.6. Form DSP 71, "Affidavit of Identifying Witness"

C5.2.1.7. Form DSP 82, "Application for Passport by Mail"

C5.2.1.8. Form DSP 1832, "Passport Application Transmittal"

C5.2.1.9. DSP Form M-343, "Notice to Applicant Concerning Birth Records"

C5.2.2. The DoS shall supply the Department of Defense the necessary stock of DSP Forms. All DoS forms are available through normal publications channels. If additional forms are needed, contact the appropriate OPR. Questions concerning DoS forms may be directed to Director, General Services Branch, Bureau of Consular Affairs, 2201 C Street, NW, Washington, DC 20520. In overseas areas, forms may be obtained from U.S. Consular Offices or Embassies.

## C5.3. REQUIRED DoD AND DoS PUBLICATIONS

C5.3.1. The DoS Passport Agent's Manual (reference (b)), should be provided to each DoD military passport agent when he or she is designated. Copies of reference (b) are available through the Service OPRs.

C5.3.2. The DoD FCG (reference (c)), is the authority for travel clearance requirements and identification for DoD personnel and their family members to enter foreign countries on official business. Reference (c) consists of a General Information Book, 4 Regional Books, and a classified supplement that encompasses every geographical location of the world. A blue plastic cover binder is available upon request. Reference (c) should be accessible to passport agents. See Chapter 1., section C1.7., for the use of reference (c). Reference (c) is continuously updated by electronic messages (ICN--Interim Change Notice) and by changes (FCCN--Foreign Clearance Change Notices) printed on a quarterly basis. Reference (c) is not available through the normal publication distribution channels. To obtain a copy write to: Defense Mapping Agency (DMA), ATTN: OCIJ,D67, 4600 Sangamore Road, Bethesda, MD, 20816-5003. FAX: DSN 287-3095, Commercial (301) 227-3095. Allow 4 weeks for delivery. Telephone inquiries may be addressed to the Defense Mapping Agency at DSN: 287-2495, Commercial (301) 227-2495 (choose option six). Requests must contain the following:

C5.3.2.1. Be on official letterhead.

C5.3.2.2. Specify the initial issuance and automatic distribution of the general information and regional booklets. Also, state whether the classified supplement is required. If the classified supplement is required, the availability of proper classified storage must also be stated in the request.

C5.3.2.3. Number of copies. Specify whether blue plastic binder is required.

C5.3.2.4. A short justification of the requirement.

C5.3.2.5. DMA account number or a request to open an account.

C5.3.2.6. Name and telephone number of a point of contact.

C5.3.2.7.  Complete mailing address of where reference (c) is to be sent (no personal names).